Crisis in America:

Families in Need

Karen V. Kitt

authorHOUSE®

AuthorHouse™
1663 Liberty Drive, Suite 200
Bloomington, IN 47403
www.authorhouse.com
Phone: 1-800-839-8640

First published by AuthorHouse 6/16/2008

ISBN: 978-1-4343-2809-0 (sc)

Library of Congress Control Number: 2008901657

Printed in the United States of America
Bloomington, Indiana

This book is printed on acid-free paper.

Unless otherwise noted, all Scripture quotations are from the King James Version / Amplified Bible Parallel Edition. Copyright 1995, by The Zondervan Corporation and the Lockman Foundaton. Publishers, Inc.

Dictionary definitions have been taken from The American Heritage Dictionary of the English Language: New College Edition. Copyright 1978, by Houghton Mifflin Company Publishers, Inc.

"Never doubt that a small group of committed citizens can change the world. Indeed, it's the only thing that ever has."

Margaret Mead

For the children......

Contents

Introduction... ix

Chapter One:
The Case for a "Call to Crisis" 1

Chapter Two:
The Case For "A New America" 5

Chapter Three:
Reverse the Curse: Owning Our Predicament 11

Chapter Four:
The Mis-education of the Negro:
Our Unique Dilemma... 17

Chapter Five:
Forgiveness, Repentance,
Redemption, Restoration: Recompense 35

Chapter Six:
The Family Home as the Key Component in the
Generational Development Cycle 45

Chapter Seven:
Working With Schools to Obtain Academic Success 59

Chapter Eight:
The Watching Remnant... 65

Notes 77

Introduction

"I will stand upon my watch, and set me upon the tower, and will watch to see what he will say unto me, and what I shall answer when I am reproved.

And the Lord answered me, and said, Write the vision, and make *it* plain upon tables, that he may run that readeth it.

For the vision *is* yet for an appointed time, but at the end it shall speak, and not lie: though it tarry, wait for it; because it will surely come, it will not tarry.

Behold, his soul *which* is lifted up is not upright in him: but the just shall live by his faith."

Habakkuk 2:1-4 KJV

This book is a love letter to the adults and particularly, the parents of America. I did not choose to write it. It was my destiny. I weep when I see the children of today, bearing the obvious physical and emotional scars of abuse and neglect brought on by parents who are absent, addicted, confused and defeated. I wail when I observe that of the many adults who are aware of their plight, very few are convicted to the point of responding to the children's cries for help.

Many Americans believe that their responsibility to others is abdicated due to the rigorous daily demands of maintaining their households and effectively raising their own children. While this reasoning might seem valid and logical on the surface, I would like to challenge your thinking. I am alerting you to the possibility that if you are not consciously involved in the struggle of a greater reality, a greater nation or at least a greater community for all—you and everything that you care for may be at risk of failure.

How many of you reading this book would identify themselves as Christians? Have you accepted Jesus Christ as your Savior and Lord? Do you serve a mighty, sovereign, everlasting, faithful God? Do you believe that He lives in and through His Holy Spirit, the third person of the Holy Trinity? If you answered these questions in the affirmative, you should be living (or working on living) a powerful Spirit-filled life, because the Christian, Spirit-filled life, according to the Word of God, should be characterized by a people who are active, abundant, and victorious! You have been given the assignment to advance the Kingdom of God against the creeping trends of confusion, mediocrity, the disregard for and resistance to authority pervading our culture. You have been given the assignment to make a difference in the lives of children in America, and yes, the world.

Like so many African-Americans who are mature adults today, I was fortunate to have parents and caregivers during the era of my childhood who attempted to provide a loving environment with a degree of stability. They stressed the importance of education and advancement. These adults also worked to instill within me the characteristics of: discipline, pride, confidence, compassion and a sense of purpose, despite the challenges presented by adolescent development in a world that was sometimes turbulent and always transforming. I am thankful for their selfless behavior and I thank God that they carried out their task with purpose, hope and a destiny in their hearts.

Unfortunately, many young people today cannot make the claim that I am able to make. America's children in need do not solely consist of the "extreme" cases of abuse and neglect that we read about in the daily newspapers or watch on the nightly news. I propose that the prevailing numbers of children in need consist of children who might be in your living room right now watching television, those who are in your morning Sunday School Class, or even those who ride to school everyday with your children.

Our children's spirits and souls are at risk in this nation. Stability, discipline, love, compassion, confidence, hope and purpose are absent in too many of our children's daily lives. Whether or not you are actively engaged, we are fighting a war-perhaps a final conflict-for the spiritual growth, survival and advancement of a generation of young people in America.

If you are alarmed, challenged or offended by these statements, read on…

Karen V. Kitt, M.Ed.

"Wisdom is the principal thing; therefore get wisdom:

and with all thy getting get understanding."

Proverbs 4:7 KJV

Chapter One:
The Case for a "Call to Crisis"

Crisis (kri'sis) n., *pl-***ses** (-sez)

1. a. A crucial point or situation in the course of anything; turning point.
    b. An unstable condition in political, international, or economic affairs in which an abrupt or decisive change is impending.

2. *Pathology.* A sudden change in the course of an acute disease, either toward improvement or deterioration.

3. The point in a story or drama at which hostile forces are in the tensest state of opposition.

4. [Latin from Greek *krisis*, turning point, from *krinein*, to separate, decide.]

Millions of adolescent children awake in America and go to school each day. A small number of them have taken the time to bathe properly, dress themselves and eat a nutritious meal. They have pleasant conversations with parents or responsible caretakers, and arrive at school on time with their assignments completed and the necessary materials for the day ahead.[1]

For this small segment of the adolescent population, their minds are focused on the academic and social challenges that will be presented in the day ahead. These students are sometimes apprehensive, but more often optimistic, confident, and competent.[2]

This book serves to address the millions of adolescents that **do not** fit the profile: students who are chronically absent or tardy; those whose stomachs are empty of food, or whose breath smells of sugared candies and soda pop at 8:00 A. M. More often than not, these same students periodically have poor hygiene, are unable to attend or consistently follow classroom rules. These older children often display behaviors that are not currently considered "age appropriate for adolescents", and are frequently the source of classroom disruptions.[3] They represent the majority of suspensions and expulsions that are incurred as consequences for inappropriate school behavior.

Unfortunately, many of these students do not achieve academic success in school, as measured by: poor grades, repeated failures, and a high drop out rate. The dilemma is not: "What shall we do about America's adolescent poor?" A significant percentage of these under- performing students come from homes that would be classified as working-middle, middle, and sometimes even upper-middle class families.[4]

While school districts and communities across America race to increase academic standards, provide interventions, hire and maintain competent teaching staffs and personnel, a growing majority of the student population is beginning to demonstrate poor performance on literacy or reading measures and evidence inadequate math, science and problem solving skills. In addition to poor school performance, more and more families and communities are struggling with difficult and inconsistent social behaviors of adolescents at home and in the community.[5]

Teachers' grade books reflect excessive numbers of incomplete and missing assignments despite frequent parent conferences, phone calls from teachers to the home, notes written back and forth in student plan books, and a myriad of other interventions that seek to communicate with the adolescent student and their families.

These interventions seek to alert students and their families of the important work that must be done, and encourage rewards and consequences (both at home and at school) for successful "student behaviors". What can we then say? The "problem" still exists. *Many of our adolescents are still literally not "making the grade!"*[6]

I propose that we are pursuing a "new" problem in America. The phenomenon is so insidious that it is overlooked as a possible growing trend. It has much to do with the way our families, industries, communities, and society have evolved during the emergence of the information age and the explosive prosperity culture that has swept our country in recent decades.

Chapter Two:
The Case For "A New America"

Proverbs of Solomon:

"Where *there* is no vision, the people perish: but he that keepeth the law, happy *is* he."

Proverbs 29:18 KJV

"Where there is no vision [no redemptive revelation of God], the people perish; but he who keeps the law [of God, which includes that of man]---blessed (happy, fortunate, and enviable) is he."

Proverbs 29: 18 Amplified

Few citizens will deny that "*much has changed in a few short years*". In the past three decades our American society has endured sweeping fundamental changes across all segments and measures of society. Consider for a moment how significant changes in the following arenas have impacted **your life** or the life of your **family members** in the past three decades: political/judicial, economic/industrial/environmental, information/technological, medical/biological, vocational/educational, social/familial, and athletic/entertainment.

Need some help? We have evolved from: concerns about a cold war, to a post-cold war, to terrorism; from space exploration and space travel to space stations; from segregation and desegregation to integration; from the industrial age to the information age; from stock market crash to stock market boom, bust and recovery; from job security to job uncertainty; from "made in America" to made anywhere else but America; from fully funded and protected retirement plans to pension plan and health insurance dissolutions without notice.

We have endured the cycles of Black Power, Women's rights, affirmative action, gay rights, new age and evangelical movements. Now we are unsure as a society, at this time, what constitutes a marriage...

This brief list of contemporary historical events has precipitated a significant and permanent transformation of the average American citizen's daily behavior, experiences, and opportunities. On the surface, we appear to have survived these great transformations in tact, however, I suggest that a great price has been paid for our nation's tremendous growth, advancement and prosperity. America suffers from inordinate rates of infant mortality, violent crimes, hunger, medically uninsured adults and children, divorce, child and adolescent obesity, depression, anxiety, and struggles with issues of self-worth.[1]

We now have at least one generation that has been raised in a post-desegregation, post-affirmative action, post-evangelical, gender-nonspecific, non-affilial society. Many of these young Americans have enlisted in the military, already given their lives, and altered their futures in service to our country. We respectfully recognize their contributions, and also celebrate the accomplishments and hopeful futures of the many other young American men and women who embody excellence, leadership, and integrity. Unfortunately, a growing number of other adolescents and young adults in America do not have access to the human, economic, and educational resources enjoyed by previous generations. A disproportionate number of these young people happen to be African-American.

Can we blame the plight of these young people on an American socio-economic, political, and judicial system that historically disenfranchised their forefathers (and mothers)? Certainly we could, however, we have remained in this posture for several decades. We can no longer afford to be helpless victims who resort to the tactic of blaming "the establishment" for institutional structures and practices that exclude and debilitate them. We are not victims. We are survivors. ***We are more than conquerors!*** (Romans, Chapter 8)

Our ancestors survived the Middle Passage, endured the most brutal form of enslavement in contemporary history, obtained emancipation, struggled through Reconstruction, marched, fought, voted and died so that we could enjoy the current day privileges to seek employment, establish businesses, choose where we live, participate in the voting process, and obtain a higher education.   This present generation must now "see" themselves as a people with a legacy, a purpose, a mission; united under a common vision and then, by faith, move to action. Yes, the task seems overwhelming, but be encouraged. <u>Active</u> faith is central to our legacy as African-Americans and believers in Christ Jesus. (Hebrews 11).

So, what do we do now? We do what we can, where we can; roll up the proverbial shirt sleeves and get to work!

Chapter Three:
Reverse the Curse:
Owning Our Predicament

The Lord's promise to Solomon:

"If my people, which are called by my name, shall humble themselves, and pray, and seek my face, and turn from their wicked ways; then will I hear from heaven, and will forgive their sin, and will heal their land. Now mine eyes shall be open, and mine ears attend unto the prayer that is made in this place."

2 Chronicles 7:14-15 KJV

Everybody seems to be looking for the hero who will save the African-American population. I know where you can find him: look in the mirror. Our destiny in America is not rooted in the work or accomplishments of a single charismatic individual but in the diligence, perseverance, integrity, and collective vision of each citizen. We have developed a victim mentality characterized by an attitude of helplessness, a learned dependency, complacency about our situation, and ignorance of the plentiful resources available to transform our present situation.

I do not criticize this collective mentality. Consider the historical roots of a people <u>forced</u> to immigrate to a foreign country and labor under the cruel system of enslavement practiced in America for over two hundred years. Add to these conditions the ensuing struggle for restoration and assimilation following emancipation the next two hundred years within an environment of disenfranchisement characterized by institutionalized racism.

Finally, combine these historical factors with the contemporary collective "exhale" that occurred during America's prosperity of the 1980s and 1990s. African Americans did not want to be burdened with the toil of advocacy and collective advancement. (Can you really blame them?) Unfortunately our "collective exhale" has placed us at risk! We now awaken, as does all America, to a "crisis" in the new millennium.

It is time for America's adult population to grow up and shake off the victim mentality that has burdened us for so long. Most of us have suffered injustice, endured emotional hardships, or labored within dysfunctional primary relationships. It is now time to "do the work" of acknowledging the pain, and seek reconciliation and healing so that our children will have a better future. Their concerns are everyone's responsibility, whether or not one thinks that one is directly affected by these trends. A nation cannot prosper and compete globally when a large number of the population is angry, ill-equipped, unmotivated, disenfranchised, illiterate, unskilled, and uneducated.

I challenge you to take the time to consider what is happening in <u>your</u> sphere of influence and decide to become more aware. Then choose a cause or a simple activity and get involved! When was the last time that you stepped into a high school or middle school building to attend an assembly, sat in on or assisted with a classroom lesson, or just observed the behavior in the hallways? You might be surprised!

"Our lives begin to end the day we become silent about the things that matter."

Dr. Martin Luther King, Jr.

Chapter Four:
The Mis-education of the Negro: Our Unique Dilemma

Educate (ej oo kat') *v.* –cated, -cating, -cates.

Transitive:
1. To provide with knowledge or training, especially through formal schooling; teach.
2. To provide with training for some particular purpose: *educate someone for the priesthood.*
3. To provide with information; inform.
4. To discipline, train or develop (taste or skill, for example).

Intransitive:
1. To teach or instruct a person or group: *Their purpose is to educate through the use of visual aids.*

See Synonyms at **teach.** [Middle English, *educaten,* from the Latin *educare,* to bring up, educate.

Education (ej oo ka' sh n) *n.* Abbreviation: ed., educ.

1. The act or process of imparting knowledge or skill; systematic instruction; teaching.
2. The obtaining of knowledge or skill through such a process; schooling.
3. a. The knowledge or skill obtained or developed by such a process; learning.
   b. A program of instruction of a specified kind or level: *driver education, a college education.*
4. The field of study that is concerned with teaching and learning: the theory of teaching; pedagogy.

The System of Education in America: Our Historical Context

A brief survey of the history of education is necessary at this time. We must look back and evaluate our past, examine and assess today's reality, and with diligence, plan for our tomorrow.

Many Americans often forget, or simply do not know, that the system of education in America originally excluded women and people of color. Principally the male children of wealthy landowners, industrialists, and businessmen received access to private schools and a variety of private tutoring methods to obtain a formal education. A formal education was virtually unobtainable, a mere dream to the commoner. These young men were often trained for specific trades under the apprenticeship method. Under the brutal system of enslavement in America, it was illegal to educate the African.

From Slavery to Reconstruction

The African was legally declared "not fully human" under the American system of enslavement and as such was demoted to the position of "chattel." They were legally bought, sold, and/or traded in the marketplace as a "labor source" to fund the enormous agricultural trade that served as the foundation of our United States of America. Geographically certain states and industries, primarily the agriculturally driven Southern states and the financial and insurance industries that supported them, became extremely rich and economically powerful.

White citizens who did not directly benefit (financially) from the slave trade, or who found its enslavement of human beings unbiblical and morally repugnant, began to organize. Abolitionist societies began to spring up and mobilize a conscience among the people throughout the Americas.

The United States declined into a state of "disunion." The nation was divided in its philosophies about who should control a young nation's vast wealth and the moral price that might have to be paid in future generations and the hereafter. As eleven Confederate states seceded from the Union, the nation declined into a state of Civil War. Utterly destroyed from within, the nation found itself in a state of "Reconstruction."

Congress passed the Thirteenth Amendment, abolishing slavery, which was ratified on December 18, 1865. **It became legal to educate the African!** Hundreds of schools were created for the purpose of educating the freedman. Teacher-training institutions and colleges were established as well. In fact, some learning institutions were co-funded by the *Freedman's Bureau*, an agency created by the United States Government to address the problems of poverty, unemployment, poor medical care and the education of the freedmen.[1]

Unfortunately resistance to the advancement of newly freed slaves was not abated by these measures. During that same year, 1865, many Southern states passed laws called "The Black Codes." Essentially, these laws restricted the ability of the newly freed slaves to marry, own property, obtain gainful employment, own or control land, or operate a business. The Civil Rights Act of 1866 was specifically legislated to eliminate these injustices and attempt to provide freedman and all blacks the full rights and privileges of American citizenship.

As we struggled to obtain a rudimentary education in poorly funded schools, the battle for basic citizenship—the legal declaration of our humanity—continued. The Fourteenth Amendment to the Constitution, passed in 1865 and ratified in 1868, sought to "provide blacks with citizenship and guaranteed that federal and state laws applied equally to blacks and whites."[2]

Later, in 1870, the right to vote was legislated through the Fifteenth Amendment to the Constitution. For a short time, blacks enjoyed the right to vote and serve in political office. Laws, however, do not govern the hearts of men. Many states created laws that *continued* to exclude blacks from the voting process and deny them the opportunity to serve in political office.[3]

The entire nation, undergoing reconstruction, staggered forward to retool itself from an economic system fueled by a massive unpaid labor force to one supplied by a labor force of wage-earners. Economies of both the North and the South enjoyed benefits from the enslavement of Africans. The abolition of the legalized slave trade dismantled many fortunes yet created many financial opportunities. Lifestyles in America were radically transformed.

System (sis' t m) *n.*

1. **A group of interacting, interrelated, or interdependent elements forming or regarded as forming a collective entity.**
2. **A functionally related group of elements**, as:
   a. The human body regarded as a functional physiological unit.
   b. A group of physiologically complementary organs or parts.
   c. A group of interacting mechanical or electrical components.
   d. A network or structures and channels, as for communications, travel or distribution.
3. A structurally or anatomically related group of elements or parts.
4. **A set of interrelated ideas, principles, rules, procedures, laws or the like.**
5. **A social, economic, or political organizational form.**
6. A naturally occurring group of objects or phenomena.
7. A set of objects pr phenomena grouped together for classification or analysis.
8. **The state or condition of harmonious, orderly interaction.**

----**See** Synonyms at **method**. [Late Latin *sytema*, from Greek *sustema*, a composite whole, from *sunistani,* to bring together, combine: *sun-*, together+*histan*i, to cause to stand.

The Rise of Industrialization and the System of Public Education

During the transition from an agricultural economy to an industrial economy, *children* became the source of cheap labor that America exploited. Youth protection policies forced employers to remove school-age children from hazardous work environments. A mandated public school system emerged that mirrored the organization and regimentation of the efficiently managed factories of the 1940s.[4]

Students traveled through hallways in quiet, well-ordered lines, moving only at the sound of a bell system. Classrooms were neatly arranged in uniform rows of desks. The teacher's desk, at the front of the room, often with the teacher sitting behind it, symbolized supreme authority. The teacher always received respect from his/her pupils.

The original public educational institutions served to shape the intellectual capacity of our citizenry, but they also imparted value systems that complemented, supported, and structured our republic, its industrial growth, and its wealth-building potential. Visionaries like John Dewey, Carter G. Woodson, Booker T. Washington, and W.E. B. DuBois spent their lifetime engaged in the study of instructional methods, the system of education and its purpose and impact upon society, and specifically the role of the newly educated black citizen in America.

By the 1940s African-American citizens had gained access to education, but the quality of the education provided to African Americans under the "separate but equal" doctrine was often inferior to that obtained by white citizens. Arguments continued as to the role or purpose education should play in the life of the African American and his ability to function and prosper in the newly industrialized (but segregated) economy.[5]

The persistence of a "colored" people hungry for knowledge resulted in a landmark court case: *"Brown v. Board of Education"*, which had to be argued before the Supreme Court of the United States of America. The world watched as the African American pressed his claim as a citizen with the right to access "equitable education."[6]

The NAACP Legal Defense Fund team, led by Thurgood Marshall, represented the plaintiffs in their suit aimed at eradicating the "Separate but Equal doctrine" that had been practiced in America since the 1870s.

Marshall's team implemented a brilliant legal strategy that petitioned the testimonies of husband-and-wife African-American psychologists and researchers Dr. Kenneth B. Clark and Dr. Mamie Phipps Clark, graduates of

Columbia University's PhD program in psychology (in the 1940s). Their study of African-American school-age children provided the necessary documentation of the <u>devastating psychological impact </u>of discrimination upon children of African descent in American culture.[7]

In 1954 the Supreme Court of the United States ruled that racial disparities (differences) in educational opportunities <u>did</u> in fact exist and that these disparities <u>must</u> be eliminated—throughout the land.[8]

<u>The world watched as the African American's right to access an "equitable education" emerged.</u> A new cycle of white violence and resistance to federal laws exploded. However, the government that once enslaved the African diligently reinforced the federal legislation of justice—access to an equal education—even using military means when necessary. Praise God!

Education in the "New America"

Our American system of public education functioned through a series of world wars, military conflicts, and cultural evolutions. African Americans attended college in record numbers, gained entry into corporate America, started businesses, and became active participants and leaders in the political process.

Education was considered an opportunity for advancement by all: a stepping stone to generational wealth. Parents raised their children to come to school with an <u>attitude of respect</u> for the institution of learning and the "keepers of the dream," the educators. In addition, only the most poverty-stricken family would send its child to school without the necessary pencils, erasers, notebooks, or paper to complete the class work required on any given school day.

Unfortunately, in the "new" America, the student demeanor of readiness, preparation, respect, or an "attitude of gratitude" is not as evident in today's typical urban classroom. Large numbers of urban students come to class without a writing utensil, not because they suffer economically, but because they are making a statement. For some students this behavior communicates that **education is no longer established as a legacy that has been instilled in them at home or in their respective communities.** They do not value the education process. Preparation, for life or for the classroom, is not a priority.

Sadly, for many students, the lack of academic preparation at school (class work) or at home (homework) communicates another important statement: **"The current system of education-school- is not relevant to their daily lives."** Increasing numbers of America's adolescents are being raised in circumstances (e.g., extreme poverty, drug and sexual abuse, divorce and separation, chronic family illness, unavailable healthcare, and just plain old "riotous living") that are "challenging" at best.

Whatever the reason, many of our young people do not verbalize or demonstrate a sense of self-worth, let alone family pride and a sense of destiny or purpose. **They simply do not carry within them, a dream—or "the village" has failed to provide an environment where their dreams can be conceived, carried to term, and birthed.**

The painful irony is that we are faced with this crisis in a "new America," where our citizens are living better than Americans have lived at any other time in history! As our nation has matured, becoming more prosperous, we have witnessed the erosion of previously esteemed values: individual contribution and sacrifice for the greater good; accountability, integrity, pride in workmanship, servanthood, excellence. Poverty and class division are a growing concern. Allegations of discrimination are on the rise. Few voices can be heard, diligently crying out to our American citizens, "Be informed, educate, activate, speak out, get involved!"[9]

● ●

Events of the new millennium year, 2001, documented a "shift" in our thinking as Americans. The terrorist attack on September 11, 2001 (911) shook us out of our revelry and brought us to our knees in unified prayer!

As we more commonly reported feelings of fear, powerlessness, depression, and burnout, a book entitled *The Purpose Driven Life (Zondervan, 2002)* was published. The author, minister Rick Warren, addressed man's sense of fear and "lack of purpose." Warren pointed the world to God's Word, the Bible, for answers. *The Purpose Driven Life: What On Earth Am I Here For?* became a best-seller on the *New York Times* list. The book jacket boasts that more than one million copies of the text have been sold! Certainly the world was hungry for answers to some very important questions.

Another important event signaling a "shift" in our thinking was the decision made by a bipartisan group of legislators to implement a solution for the disparities in academic achievement among students of various racial, ethnic, gender, and socio-economic populations. The No Child Left Behind Act (NCLB), signed by President George W. Bush on January 8, 2002, imposed an unprecedented mandate of accountability upon school districts across America.

The NCLB Act was drafted upon one "simple" concept: "If a child is in a classroom, being instructed for one year, then at the end of that year he/she should have obtained one year of academic achievement in the areas of his/her instruction." How do we determine if the goal has been met? We test the students in the content areas where they have received instruction during the school year. If learning has taken place, a student's performance (test scores) should indicate that one year of learning (student achievement) has taken place.[10]

While this thinking certainly sounds reasonable, the NCLB Act generated a lot of controversy. Some critics charged that the act might incite an environment of "blaming" teachers and school officials for the lack of student achievement. Others expressed concern that the use of tests was unreliable or that students would suffer from excessive testing. Many expressed concern about the government's need to fund professional development programs for teachers, purchase and maintain state-of-the-art technology and instructional materials, lower class sizes, and address the needs of students in special-education programs.

Despite the fact that adequate funding was never approved or disbursed to accomplish the 2002 mandate to boost student achievement, many gains in student achievement *have* taken place across our nation. Our educators, our families, and our children are to be commended on the Herculean efforts taken to obtain the gains that have been made in the interest of our children and our nation's progress.[11]

Accountability in any field (e.g., politics, religion, business, medicine) is an arduous practice, but the contribution of accountability practices toward the preservation of integrity, excellence, and equity in any professional field is undeniable.

Under the "new" system of education in the "new America," parents exercised their right to take their children out of the public school system and place them in alternative schools. Many of these parents quickly learned how difficult it is to operate a safe and effective school. They learned that the public funds that flow into the existing local public school district, although substantial, are very necessary. Building maintenance and operation, technical and human resources are essential but very costly. These resources must be managed by people with vision and integrity, under a system of quality, efficiency, and accountability, as would be required in any successful enterprise or industry.

Instead of dismantling the public school system, consider walking in your anointing and authority as a believer. Bombard the gates of America's education system with prayer and your presence. Stand up for the instruction that you want to see in your child's classroom: content area, civics, and values. Teach your children to be informed consumers of knowledge. You become the advocate for your child. Defend your family's right to choose to live by Christian principles both in your home and in your community! Get involved![12]

Remember:
The proverbial squeaky wheel gets the grease!

Family Checklist to Overcome Mis-education

____ 1. Get informed. Purchase a copy of the book: *The Mis-education of the Negro* by Carter G. Woodson. Read the book and discuss it with your spouse, adult family members, close friends, and finally your school-age children. You will be astounded to learn that many of the concerns expressed by Carter G. Woodson more than seventy years ago still ring true today!

____ 2. Educate yourself and your family. Conduct internet searches and check out library books and view videos using these key phrases: Reconstruction Era, Black Codes, Jim Crow, segregation, Plessy v. Ferguson, "Separate but Equal", Brown v. Board of Education, "No Child Left Behind."

____ 3. Declare that "education is and will continue to be a priority in your household." Have a family meeting. Set clear age-appropriate goals for each family member. Post them in a central place and refer to them on a regular basis (weekly, monthly, etc.). Design a reward system for individual and family progress!

___ 4. Set the example.

Prayer for Healing and Deliverance from Mis-education under our System of Education in America

Dear Lord,

Open the eyes of my understanding so that I can see things as you see them. Give me divine wisdom and understanding of what it means to teach others and to be taught by wise counselors.

Lord, thank you for the gifts that you have given me. Help me celebrate the gifts, skills, and talents that you have given me. Show me how to benefit others. Give me the courage to strengthen areas where I need improvement by reading, getting training, and attending specialized workshops and classes, or even enrolling in a formal program of higher education.

Grant me favor as I pursue excellence and seek to walk in my calling. Equip me to be an advocate for my child, children in my family, and the children in my community.

In the mighty name of Jesus, I declare emancipation for myself, my household, my family, and my community. I declare that I am (we are) free of generational curses and throw off any hindrances from the past.

I declare in Jesus's name that I (we) will no longer be "miseducated." I forgive those who told me I was stupid, unskilled, and inferior. I forgive and release those who told me (in word or deed) that I would never amount to anything.

I forgive <u>myself</u> for not taking advantage of learning opportunities that were extended to me. I forgive <u>myself</u> for not believing in myself. I forgive <u>myself</u> for any poor choices that I made in my life that now cause me pain and hardship, or place me at a disadvantage.

I walk in self-love and self-appreciation. I awake daily with enthusiasm, expecting income, employment, and financial opportunities to come to me. I gladly receive these gifts from above and manage them with godly wisdom and integrity.

Now, Lord, bless me indeed! Enlarge my territory. Take me (and my loved ones) into financial increase. Open doors to higher employment, raises, and promotions that no man can shut. Grant me favor when I find myself before those in authority.

Father, I know that you designed me for greatness. Fill my mind with <u>your</u> plan and <u>your</u> purpose for my life. Increase my wisdom. Increase my knowledge and understanding of kingdom principles. Increase my hunger for <u>your</u> truth and righteousness. Enlarge my capacity to receive your blessings. Protect me from all harm. Place a hedge of protection around me, my family, my businesses, and my possessions, in Jesus' name.

I praise you in advance for what you are doing for me (us) now. I bless your mighty name and give you the glory! This I pray In Jesus' name.

Amen

Chapter Five:
Forgiveness, Repentance, Redemption, Restoration: Recompense

"But ye shall be named the **Priests of the Lord**; *men* shall call you the **Ministers of our God**: ye shall eat the riches of the Gentiles, and in their glory shall ye boast yourselves.

For your shame *ye shall have* double; and *for* confusion they shall rejoice in their portion: therefore in their hand they shall possess the double: everlasting joy shall be unto them.

For I the Lord love judgment, I hate robbery for burnt offering; and I will direct their work in truth, and I will make an everlasting covenant with them.

And their seed shall be known among the Gentiles. And their offspring among the people: all that see them shall acknowledge them, that they are the seed *which* the Lord hath blessed.

I will greatly rejoice in the Lord, my soul shall be joyful in my God; for he hath clothed me with the garment of salvation, he hath covered me with the robe of righteousness, as a bridegroom decketh *himself* with ornaments, and as a bride adorneth *herself* with jewels.

For as the earth bringeth forth her bud, and as the garden causeth the things that are sown in it to spring forth; so the Lord God will cause righteousness and praise to spring forth before all the nations."

Isaiah 61: 6-11 KJV

The African American, so despised by men, has an assignment of redemptive work before him. This is our assignment as a people on the earth. To seek redemption and recompense from the hands of an oppressor is illogical and unbiblical. Even Moses, under God's instruction, sought release for his people. But God "hardened Pharaoh's heart" and release was not obtained until God intervened supernaturally (Exodus 11 and 12). The former slaves walked out of Egypt carrying the wealth of their oppressors (Exodus 12:35,36). The Lord God did it once. He will do it again! He is waiting on us to position ourselves to receive the promises of restoration and recompense.

How will this be accomplished?

Step One: We must revive salvation/evangelism in our communities.

The church must return to its original mandate of saving souls. We have enjoyed a period of erecting massive church buildings, remodeling and renovating beautiful structures in the name of the Lord. It is a good thing. However, in what is known as "The Great Commission" (Matthew 28:16-20; Luke 24:36-49; John 20:19-23; Acts 1:6-8), Jesus instructed his disciples to go out with power and authority, make believers of men and women, and teach them the ways of the kingdom of God. We have experienced a much-needed time of education and preparation in the present era. Now we must strategically get out of the pews and back into the public domain to evangelize the thousands that do not know Jesus Christ as Savior and Lord.

Step Two: We must organize prayer vigils, rallies, and worship services dedicated to teach forgiveness, speak forgiveness, and engage in prophetic acts of forgiveness and redemption.

When God's written word on forgiveness and redemption are taught, studied, spoken, and mixed with faith, forgiveness will manifest in our hearts, collective healing will take place, and forgiveness will begin to manifest itself in the earth. We <u>can</u> forgive our oppressors and those who hate us. In fact, when we lay hold of forgiveness, we will begin to sow seeds of redemption, but the work will not yet be complete.

The seeds of redemption are planted in forgiveness, but like all seeds, they will only flourish in good ground. Seeds of forgiveness manifest themselves as redemption among a people when the people joyously live a consecrated lifestyle of holiness and humility before the Lord. The redeemed remnant is aware of and walks in authority as *Priests of the Lord* and *Ministers of our God in the Earth*. They then progress and operate as *Kings* in the earth. They frame their world with their words. They order their world with their words! My people, African

Americans, we must repent of our sins as a people and seek God! The universal timing of manifestation of the supernatural power of God is here *now*. We must walk in our kingdom authority wherever we find ourselves, empowered to engineer our own future.

Step Three: While we rally for forgiveness of our enemies and look to God for manifested redemption, we must *strategically* fast and engage in prayer meetings, rallies, and dedicated worship services to fight for our families, our children, our communities, our possessions, and our enterprises.

In other words, we must come into our kingdom anointing, make war against the enemy, and frame our world using God's Word. We must (corporately) speak what we desire to see made manifest in our lives.

Step Four: We must conduct prayer rallies for debt release, prosperity, and the wisdom to manage it. We must throw off mindless consumption and instead consciously vote with our dollars and make demands as kingdom people for kingdom initiatives in the earth. We must collectively and consistently pray for the revelation of God's kingdom to be released upon the earth.

I believe that great gains can be accomplished in *this generation* if we grasp who we are in God and realize the times and seasons in which we now live. Our children must be taught to be kingdom-minded and trained to be kingdom warriors.

We cannot be released to prosper and receive our recompense until our *collective* spiritual work has been performed. The earth will continue to "groan" until this work is completed by a remnant within the remnant (Romans 8). When we begin to take steps of progress and walk in kingdom purpose, the glory of the Lord will begin to be revealed in and through the lives of believers.

God has already released a "breaker anointing" in the earth. This anointing, or divine empowerment, manifests when God recognizes an individual or group of individuals who are fed up with bondage or injustice, seek the Lord, hear His words, and know with certainty in their minds and hearts that it is God's will and God's timing (now) to break through the injustices and establish His righteousness. Thy kingdom come in the earth.[1]

We are uniquely positioned—as believers, as the global church, as a nation, as people of color—for perhaps the greatest manifestation of the glory of God this present generation has ever seen. It will be a supernatural, trans-generational blessing—an empowerment to prosper that will transform the world as we know it! God's people will be whole: nothing missing, nothing broken, lacking nothing. We will walk in the authority of the righteousness of God.

Malcolm X made a profound statement that brought fear to many and encouraged others: "The purpose of the Black man is to bring justice to the planet."[2] This statement, so packed with the potency, passion, and vision of the man who spoke it, was a seed that fell on "stony ground." When I was a young African-American girl, his words planted within me a sense of hope. I maintained a sense of wonder about how this prophetic word would come to pass—and whether it would happen in my lifetime.

I believe that Malcolm and Martin were assassinated because they <u>both</u> tapped into a prophetic realm that would have resulted in manifestation. Given the opportunity to complete their individual spiritual journeys, they might possibly have collaborated to speak a vision on one accord.

When these two prophets received the revelation of the manifestation of God's kingdom on earth at the same time-the enemy moved in to annihilate them. We didn't understand what was happening in the spirit. We were not established in our kingdom positions to intercede for them and speak a common vision.

We received a "glimpse of the glory." We saw the promised land. We even crossed over Jordan, but we have not yet possessed the land to the glory of God. We are being overrun by the giants within (greed, selfishness, jealousy, envy, strife) and without (racism, entitlement).

In the 1960s we wanted manifestation of justice, many chanted, "by any means necessary." Many were ready to arm themselves, knowing that they would march to their deaths. Other citizens, who were no less passionate or determined to see a visible change in our nation but were opposed to violence, marched under the banner of "nonviolent resistance." We didn't have a revelation of the kingdom of God within us.

We were very much like the New Testament Jews who were awaiting a Messiah to liberate them from bondage. They envisioned a fighting liberator—one whom they could touch and ingratiate to gain position and favor to further personal platforms and agendas. Instead God sent them a baby, born in a manger. He became a man "of no reputation" who carried all authority in heaven and earth. Jesus, God's only son, was the best gift God could have given.

We were so overwhelmed with the intensity and toil of the struggle for equal rights in the natural realm, that we failed to tap into a higher realm of operating in the gift, the earnest deposit, that Jesus gave us: the Holy Spirit.

Some of us had knowledge of what we might call a godly experience, but we did not have a revelation of our kingdom position, power, and authority in the earth.

As believers, we have now been well instructed in the "mystery" of how a "king" can come into the earth, subdue kingdoms, establish righteousness, and overcome evil with good. We now know and understand that the "things" we see and touch in this world are the result of what has been "spoken" in the spirit realm. We now know that as Christians, disciples of Jesus Christ, we are "speaking spirits" who are created in the image of God with authority, power, and dominion over the earth. We must now—in peace, love, and with determination—get on our faces before God, on one accord, and do what He instructs us to do.

When the scriptures speak of violence, e.g., "the kingdom suffereth violence and the violent take it by force" (Matthew 11:12), the implied action is *not* a bloody physical conflict resulting in murder. The scriptures refer to the practice of fervent, relentless prayer and individual and corporate fasting in relentless pursuit of a goal (Nehemiah, Esther, Isaiah 58:5-12,13-14).

This kind of spiritual warfare, however, can take its toll on the mind, body, spirit, and soul, but the price is well worth the victory. Again, Jesus, our example, in the garden of Gethsemane, sweat "drops like blood" as He labored in prayer before God on His way to the cross! He has already won for us the victory and is now seated at the right hand of God, forever making intercession for us. Why can't we humble ourselves and pray?

"If my people, which are called by my name, shall humble themselves, and pray, and seek my face, and turn from their wicked ways: then will I hear from heaven, and will forgive their sins and heal their land."

II Chronicles 7:14 KJV

Chapter Six:
The Family Home as the Key Component in the Generational Development Cycle

Contrary to what many parents believe, the success of their children in school is greatly influenced by: a parent's encouragement, high expectations for academic achievement; the child's *perception* that his/her parent is involved, and *actual* parental involvement in his/her child's education.[10] These factors form the building blocks for the family's effective partnership and collaboration with schools. They also make a positive contribution to children's perceptions of competency and self-worth.

Numerous studies have been conducted and there is a growing body of research to support these statements, but we need look no further than the Word of God for our reference. God's word is eternal and never-changing. The spiritual laws that God spoke and established before the foundation of the world still operate as He intended today. **We must not deceive ourselves to think that we have no influence, power, or authority over our children and our households today.**

"…A Three-Fold Cord is Not Quickly Broken"

Ecclesiastes 4:12b KJV

The circumstances and forces that we perceive to be insurmountable: the fast-paced lifestyle that drives us in the new millenium; negative relationships that compete for our children's loyalties from outside the home; information, sounds and images that bombard our children through media and technology, **are not** more powerful than Almighty God!

God created **all** things and **He gave man the mind to create** the many other things that we view and interact with in the universe. As Kingdom people, we must work to shake our mind-set from the prevailing "natural" view of our circumstances that results in a fearful, tentative reaction to our existence in the earth.

We must now <u>accept</u> our position in the Kingdom of God, adopt a "supernatural"-all things are possible--mind-set, and purposefully hasten to educate, train, and equip the Body of Christ to view our world from a Kingdom perspective. The saints must then be released to go on their way---transacting business for Kingdom advancement as it pertains to every situation in their daily lives.

"But ye are a chosen generation, a royal priesthood, a holy nation, a peculiar people: that ye should show forth the praises of him who hath called you out of darkness into his marvelous light...."

(I Peter 2:9 KJV)

The Family as Primary Learning Environment

No matter what form best describes your "family unit" e.g. single-parent male, single-parent female, divorced, separated; extended family sharing one household, adoptive or foster parent household, **you set the tone** for the learning environment (or lack thereof) that exists in your home. You are communicating your feelings and ideas about education to your child by what you choose to do and say every day.

Does your child know that learning is a priority in your household? Do they know why education is important? Do they see you reading the paper or some other form of text daily? Are you modeling the importance of learning? Do they witness the benefits of learning by watching you advance in your daily life ? Is there a variety of literature (newspapers, magazines, books) in your home for everyone to read?

The Lord instructed us to "***train up*** our children in the way that they should go; that when they are old they will not depart from it." Proverbs 22:6   Let's examine the natural *and* spiritual implication of this passage of scripture.

The **New College Edition of the New American Heritage Dictionary of the English Language** instructs us that the verb, *"to train"* means: "to coach in some mode of behavior or performance", "to make proficient with specialized instruction and practice", "to prepare physically, as with a regimen", "to cause to take a desired course or shape, as by manipulating", "to focus or direct;" "to aim." It can also mean "to draw, drag, or trail."

When we examine the noun form of the word, **"train"**, the meanings suggest people or objects that are connected; that follow along or are drawn to move in an orderly line or succession. A train is also defined as "a string of gunpowder that acts as a fuse for exploding a charge"; or a locomotive.

The **Key Word Study Bible** lexical aid to the Old Testament (pg. 1613) explains that "train up" comes from the Hebrew word, *"Chanakh"*, which means: "to initiate; to teach; to dedicate, consecrate; to inaugurate." The feminine noun, "Chanukkah" comes from this word as well, meaning "a dedicatory sacrifice, a dedication, an inauguration." It is from this feminine noun form of the word, that we obtain the "Hanukkah Feast" that is observed by followers of Jewish tradition today, in late December.

This scripture in Proverbs 22:6 is a very specific. We are charged to: sacrificially dedicate or devote; consecrate or set apart; to coach our children--at each stage of their development--to emerge as responsible, functional adults in the culture and society in which they will live.

This charge to "sacrificially dedicate"; to "coach", "teach", "focus", "direct", and prepare our youth for a "life of responsibility as an adult" is not an easy one. It requires dogged determination and self-inspection. The adult often endeavors to establish a stable, nurturing environment for their children, while modeling and prescribing positive behaviors that are closely supervised and consistently enforced.

Failure to "chanakh" or "train up" our children can result in deadly consequences. Are we not reaping the results of haphazard, inconsistent training, unconsecrated (school and family) teaching; unholy devotion and a lack of dedicatory sacrificing in the education and rearing of our children in this present age? We must repent and regroup--move quickly--to reverse what was allowed to creep in and compromise our future.

I have a few words to share with parents and caregivers of the broad age-groups in which we identify children.

Parent of infants, toddlers, and young children: You are responsible for teaching your child to read before they reach Kindergarten. You are responsible for teaching your child about nature, music, art, history, math and science in our daily world. Use videos, museums and libraries to share these subjects with them where you may not have the personal knowledge or experience. Enroll them in pre-school or head start programs. Expand your child's world for him/her. They will love you for it.

Parents of middle school and high school age children: **You are still the primary advocate of your child's academic success.** This is not the time to back off and give your children over to outside influences that you don't know, are unsure of, or even disapprove. On the contrary, this is a time to increase and improve communication with your children.

Have discussions that allow you to share your family's position on the difficult topics that we face in our world today. Support your adolescent children by helping them make informed, thoughtful decisions. Engage in problem-solving with them when they need assistance or make mistakes. Establish and communicate high expectations for their academic progress and success. Issue a few firm procedures and controls and be consistent.

Monitor your child's choices.   **Pray with and for them daily. Make daily confessions, and teach them to make daily confessions of their success.**

<u>The Family as Primary Agent of Relational Development and the Formation of a Child's Value System</u>

Parents a brief word needs to be spoken about our life and challenge as an adult living in today's world. We have financial responsibilities, occupational demands, relationship frustrations and medical challenges. Our children are watching how *we* respond to these challenges. They are making determinations, both consciously and unconsciously, about how *they* should respond to the challenges they are facing in their world right now, as adolescents, and later on as adults.

You may think that you are coping, dealing with your life challenges in a healthy manner, but I must caution you to look more closely. Many children come to school angry, depressed, or simply overwhelmed by the difficult circumstances or situations that exist in their homes. If you need assistance with a problem that is keeping you from being the best parent-teacher-trainer you can be, seek help!

Please be aware,no matter your color, ethnicity, socio-economic status, *we all have problems*. It's *the way* that you approach, walk out, and overcome your struggles: medical, depression, chronic illness, family member "off the hook".......that teach and prepare your children to effectively relate to other human beings in their world!

Your actions are teaching them how to cope with disappointment or loneliness; how to relate to individuals that are different from yourselves; how to form healthy friendships, how to become a problem-solver; how to avoid addiction and walk in hope or faith. **Your actions** teach them that it's okay to lie or cheat, steal, gamble or scheme. **You are the primary, God-ordained trainer of your children. Do you want to inaugurate them to disrespect, renounce and subvert authority; or do you want them to walk in excellence, *true* prosperity, and Kingdom leadership?**

"Train up a child in the way he should go: and when he is old he will not depart from it."

Proverbs 22:6

The Family: Imparting the Primary Vision

Dear parents: Do not underestimate your influence upon your children. Read the Bible. Pray and meditate upon your vision for your family (and community). Write the vision. Share it with your spouse and children. Agree upon a common vision. Pray over it regularly. Believe God. Walk it out, by faith!

If you do not have a vision for yourself and your children; if you don't know Jesus as Savior and Lord; if you are just so beaten down by life that you don't have the strength to look up or carry a vision; find a Bible-teaching, visionary church to attend. Become a member of a house of believers that *live* and *teach* the Word of God. Your life **will** be transformed! Your life **will** be renewed! Your children **will** prosper and be in good health! Amen!

Checklist of Effective Strategies for School Success:

- Turn off the television/video games/internet unless in use for education and learning.

- Limit the amount of telephone time during the school week e.g. Sunday P.M.-Thursday P.M. Let your adolescents "earn recreational tech time."

- Establish family reading time in your home. Read to your children. Have them read to you and to each other.

- Discuss current events in your home

- Communicate your family vision on a regular basis

- Teach your children about your occupation. They should understand the connection between what you do to earn a living and their ability to obtain food, shelter, education, comfort, recreation, etc.

- Instruct and involve them in your home economics/ your family vision

- Re-institute family meal time/chores/allowance (Our children are ignorant of capital/money management. African-Americans represent one of the nation's largest consumers, yet our children cannot calculate real world problems that include sales tax, discounts off merchandise, or making change from currency and coin. They make no connection between education and training to the cycle of savings, investment, and enterprise.)

- Establish family recreation time, yet downsize "busyness." Only engage in activities that conform to your family mission statement.

- Take advantage of the benefits of religious affiliation: you obtain an advocate; you become part of a larger vision; and you eliminate isolation. Affiliation provides nurturing and compassion; access to civil services, and quality Youth and Family Activities.

Don't give up!

<u>Prayer for Family Home as the Key Component in the Generational Development Cycle</u>

Loving Heavenly Father, I (we) come to you in the precious name of Jesus, acknowledging you as my/our Creator, the Giver of Life, the Giver of all good and perfect gifts. Lord, *you* designed the family unit, so it is to *you* that I/we come seeking wisdom and instruction about my/our family.

I humbly accept the assignment that you have given me as mother/father/grandparent/aunt/uncle/guardian to these, your children. I submit my will to you today, and place my loved ones in your all-sufficient hands. Strengthen my body, mind, and spirit to run this race with patience, dear Lord. Renew my (our) mind as I (we) read and meditate upon the Word of God.

Teach me Holy Spirit, what to say, what to do, where to go, and how to seek help when the adversary attacks the safety and unity of my (our) home. Let me (us) walk in the knowledge that your grace is sufficient to meet all of my (our) needs. I thank you that I am (we are) not alone in this fight, for you have given angels charge over me (us) lest I (we) dash my foot against a stone.

I decree that I (we) am blessed; my (our) children are blessed, and I (we) walk in the favor of God. Lord, flood our home with *your* love, *your* joy, and *your* peace that passes all understanding. Give me (us) the courage and vision to "train up my (our) children in the way that they should go, so that when they are old, they *will not* depart from it." In Jesus' name I declare that any mistakes that I (we) have made in the past are now forgiven and cast into the sea of forgetfulness, for I (we) have a new hope in Christ Jesus!

Father, I (we) thank you for giving me new and creative ways to spend more time in fellowship with my family. I (we) thank you that my (our) children hear and obey your voice wherever they are and whenever you speak. I (we) thank you for opening doors for them that cannot be shut. And I (we) thank you that doors are shut that only you can open. I (we) thank you for directing my (our) children to classrooms, worship centers, community events, and personal relationships that align with the Word of God. Open my (our) eyes Lord, so that I (we) can see what is taking place in my life (our lives), the life of my (our) children, and in my (our) home. Open my mouth Lord, so that I (we) speak your Word over every situation in our lives.

Quicken my (our) spirit dear Lord, so that I (we) recognize your voice only and operate according to *your* divine will. Teach me (us) how to communicate with: educators, health care providers, community leaders and legislators so that I (we) operate in the earth as fit, effective and godly advocate(s) for my (our) family. I declare that all family and generational dysfunctions are now **canceled** in the name of Jesus. Only divine blessings now flow in my family, from generation to generation, and generations to come, in Jesus' name I pray.

Amen

"...but as for me and my house, we will serve the Lord."

Joshua 24:15b

Chapter Seven:
Working With Schools to Obtain Academic Success

"Wherefore seeing we also are compassed about with so great a cloud of witnesses, let us run with patience the race that is set before us..."

Hebrews 12:1 KJV

"For God has not given us the spirit of fear, but of power, and of love, and a sound mind."

II Timothy 1:7 KJV

Many proactive parents face difficult decisions when working in tandem with classroom teachers and school officials to ensure the success of their children. How do we navigate the system of education to obtain success for our children? To forge a future for our families? To walk out a destiny for our people and essentially, all citizens of the world?

First we must de-mystify the meaning and implications of the "Achievement Gap" that has the American system of education so polarized. The term, 'Achievement Gap', refers to the disparity or differences in academic achievement, as demonstrated by annual test scores, between children of different racial, gender and socio-economic backgrounds. Simply stated, students belonging to so-called "minority groups" e.g. African-American, Latino, Native Peoples, greatly under-perform Caucasian students on state mandated assessments of Math, Science, Reading, and Social Studies.[1]

Even more alarming is the fact that these differences or "gaps" in achievement/school performance broaden even further when the data is "disaggregated" or broken down into smaller, "sub-groups" of populations.[2] The reading and mathematics scores of African-American males for example, are so far below the scores of African-American females, and Caucasian males and females that one begins to ask oneself "What is going on in America's classrooms? Is this particular group, African-American males, unable to learn? Are African American children and children belonging to other minority groups <u>unable</u> to learn?" Of course not!

The disparities in academic performance occur for many reasons: generational and situational poverty, family illiteracy, the declining age of first time mothers and fathers of young infants; fatherless homes, motherless homes; parents who are intimidated by the school system and/or who themselves had negative experiences or were even victimized by the system. Now forced to participate in the school-parent conferencing/communication process as parents, these individuals are resentful of or intimidated by teachers they have never even met.

Sadly, many of these parents are reluctant to advocate for their own children when they see the negative cycle re-emerging. In addition, many children in these homes do not have access to stimulating or rigorous after-school, weekend, or summer enrichment programs where their minds are challenged, their academic success is celebrated and their creativity is nurtured.

For a variety of reasons, too many Americans, across social and economic classes, carry a general lack of respect for education. We do not share "the vision" that the attainment of a quality education (not just attending school) for each citizen is fundamental to the creation and perpetuation of a productive and prosperous society.

Too often, we Americans give "lip service" to the importance of education, but in policy and practice, it is difficult to locate evidence that our nation truly "sees" and values education (and the systems necessary to support its effectiveness) as a cornerstone for building and advancing our nation. In the "new America", we have failed to unite toward the common goal of building families, communities, and our nation.

Numerous research now exists to document that children of poverty, children from various ethnic backgrounds, in fact--all children-- <u>can</u> learn and even <u>excel</u> in learning when they: are given equal access to a rigorous curriculum, are instructed by teachers who employ a variety of instructional methods and receive training and nurturing from the unified efforts of variety of stakeholders- each of whom communicates and models high expectations for the child.[3]

The legislation enacted in 2002 entitled "No Child Left Behind" (NCLB) sought to eliminate disparities and establish uniform high performance standards throughout our American system of education.[4] The Act provided benchmarks, standards, or learning outcomes for any student enrolled during a calendar school year by each subject and at each grade level. School systems, community groups, front line educators, committed students, their caregivers and families have labored greatly toward ensuring that each child in America demonstrates academic progress from one school year to the next.

Five years later we can conclude that gains have been made in the academic achievement of our youth, but the "gap" still exists.[5] Even more staggering and beyond the scope of this book, is the gap that exists between our "American" standards of achievement and the levels of academic achievement being attained by members of our global community!

My fellow Americans, brothers and sisters, I propose that the "achievement gap" will not be eliminated until we **Get Involved!** In our quest for prosperity, material gain, and personal pleasure, we have forgotten that families and children make up the key building block of our society and culture.

Go before the Lord in prayer. Ask Him what He would have you do to make a difference! When our hearts are right, we become able to make the commitment to honor and support families and children. We can become, nurture and produce individuals that are healthy, whole, and competent contributors to a great society. We must accept the challenge to become an integral part of our children's daily academic lives!

Chapter Eight:
The Watching Remnant

This book has sought to further discussion of the "system of education in America" and its impact upon African-American youth, our families, and our future. We are at a crossroads in history. Will education, a major vehicle that brought us up from slavery to franchise in this beloved country, cease to be effective for our people? The answer lies within us. We must decide and establish our priorities.

Research confirms that our kids can and do learn when given clear expectations to achieve in a non-threatening environment and when they receive recognition for their choice to achieve.[1] Historically, when given opportunity and a level playing field we not only excel, but we often dominate in whatever field we gain entry. So why do we not dominate the fields of science and technology, as well as literature, politics, entertainment and the arts?

We have not conquered the enemy in the battlefield of our "collective mind." As a people, African-Americans have had to: Overcome a historical stronghold of illiteracy and injustice (Chapter 4); Flee the seduction and entanglement with self-gratification and materialism-- the world's riches-- in the "New America" (Chapter 2); Have the faith and fortitude to move beyond the despair and hopelessness of cyclical poverty (Chapter 3); and labor for true peace--personal wholeness in our inner man (Chapter 5). We must restore the family home as the key to the generational development cycle (Chapter 6), while pushing for policies that support family educational and economic stability. We must also diligently work **with** our public schools to obtain academic success for our children (Chapter 7).

Many African-Americans *have* "done the work" to advance their academic and financial status, to be healthy and whole. Unfortunately, we --as African-American people- have not rallied to honor our human potential. We do not treat each other or honor ourselves as human beings. We are deceived and distracted by the world's values and systems. We have not yet declared and/or exercised our Biblical mandate to choose mates for the purpose of establishing stable family units wherein we can build financial wealth, enjoy emotional stability, and in turn train and educate future generations to dominate in the earth. **We have no collective purpose!**

This is not a condemnation-- but a revelation of our **unique dilemma** as the African in America. Few ethnic groups are so despised in the earth. Few ethnic groups have endured, labored, suffered and survived the massive and relentless campaigns of hatred, disenfranchisement and injustice as the African-American. Yet, we still exist! God is merciful. We are blessed.

If the African-American is to overcome injustice, it must come from within. Deliverance must come from within ourselves, as the peaceable fruit of becoming what **Christ** has called us to be. ***When we submit to God and pray: "Thy Kingdom come, thy will be done", divine deliverance will flow throughout our communities, our nation, and even our world .*** God's glory will fill the earth as we first gain precious victories over the little and then the greater.

Beloved: *Are you praying? Are you watching?*

God gave me a message in the Spring and Summer of 2004 about a "Remnant." I walked around asking everyone I knew who studied the word of God: "Do you know about the remnant?" "God is talking about a remnant." I had been taught that the Lord uses each one of us, if we yield to Him, to finish a task, to do a work for His kingdom here on earth. But, it was not until I sought and encountered his enduring, manifold presence that I fully realized and accepted that the Lord was speaking to me, as one of his "remnant" people, about the "glory of the Lord that is about to fill this earth."

It's our time. In the body of Christ, each of us has at least one task to complete. Just as "to each one of us is given the measure of faith" and as we are admonished to "stir up the gift within us", we each have <u>something</u> to do! This does not mean that each one of us will invent the cure for cancer or solve the energy crisis in America. Many will be effective fathers or mothers, teachers or pastors: crucial assignments that train and sustain generations and serve as the foundation of our culture. Until you have a clear word from the Lord about *your* particular assignment, a good place to begin is to "watch and pray" right where you are.

The bible tells us in the Old and New Testaments that "the just shall live by faith." (Habakkuk 2:4b and Hebrews 10:38a). God is on our side. He has always been on the side of the downtrodden. He hasn't changed. ("Jesus Christ the same yesterday, and today, and forever." Hebrews 13:8) With <u>active</u> faith, we must talk, walk and move in the visible to manifest the blessings that are waiting for us, unseen, in the invisible. We must trust God to make the crooked paths straight, yes, even in the new millenium.

God has an *infinite* number of ways to make things right for his covenant people. He delights in demonstrating His love and provision for his people. We only have to position ourselves as little children to receive from Him; to seek his loving presence; to learn of Him. You cannot lose when you place your trust and future with El Shaddai, the Almighty God.

Get involved in your child's educational experience! This may require you to change some priorities. Your family might have to give up one or two costly entertainment activities per month. Ask God how you can live without the 2nd or 3rd job. Trust in God. Pray.

Become a ***visible presence*** in your child's school building. Do not be intimidated. Show up with a smile--God will do the rest. Ask questions, get brochures, attend functions--plan some! Sit in on classes, attend athletic and other extra-curricular (after-school) events. The teachers will be inspired and empowered when they see a "three-fold chord" (the child/ the family/the communityschool system-Chapter 6) established and operating in their learning community.

The children *want* to see your face! They will stand taller, run faster, test better, and most importantly rise to walk in integrity, maturity and excellence knowing that someone who looks like them cares enough to get involved as advocates for their success. Children of God: **We *must* bring the American <u>system</u> of education into divine (kingdom) alignment.**

Amen

Prayer of the Remnant

Father, in the precious name of Jesus, I/We bring this nation's system of education before you today. Bind up the spirits of deception, poverty, lack, confusion, limitation, exclusion and any pedagogy that sets itself in opposition to or does not line up with the Word of God.

Father, loose the seeds of divine wisdom and Kingdom knowledge throughout our land. Let these seeds immediately find good ground in which to manifest your glory in this present generation and in future generations to come.

In Jesus' name and by the power of His shed blood on Calvary, remove all Satanic strategies and reverse all ungodly limitations that have been placed upon all people in these United States of America.

By faith we speak revival across the land! May we, your people, hunger and thirst for your presence. May we hunger and thirst for your righteousness. May we hunger for your Word. Lord, may we edify ourselves and others by speaking your Word continually. May we be known as your children by the signs and wonders that follow us. Let God arise, and let our enemies be scattered!

In Jesus's name, we speak to the angels of the Lord that watch over us. We say: "Bring forth healing to our nation. Bring forth peace and justice for all. We release angels of protection on our behalf to defeat the enemy. We trust, Holy Spirit, that you go before our children, to prepare the way."

"We unite as believers, and we declare in Jesus' name, that all of America's children will come forth as mighty men and women of God. They shall be known as a nation of priests and kings! Even now Lord God, we declare they increase in knowledge and come forth as creative scientists and inventors, skilled physicians and medical researchers, visionary titans in industry; Godly statesmen, gifted educators, and super anointed men and women of God."

When they speak life and righteousness in the earth, let the earth move to come into obedience with your Word and your will . We declare that our children hear only *your* voice, heavenly Father, and another they do not follow. Have your way dear Lord. Let your Glory fill the earth! We seal this prayer in Jesus' name. We shout the victory and we praise your holy name!

Amen

"So we built the wall; and all the wall was joined together unto the half thereof: for the people had a mind to work."

Nehemiah 4:6

Prayer of Salvation
(Read Aloud)

Dear Jesus,

Please come into my heart. Fill me with your Holy Spirit. I confess that I need you as Savior and Lord of my life.

I believe that you died for me on the cross, and that in three days you rose again with all power in your hands.

I confess that by your stripes I am healed, made whole, and set free from any and all hindrances from my past. From this moment on, I walk in total and complete victory. I have new life in Jesus Christ!

Jesus, I ask that you activate the gifts and hidden treasures that you deposited within me before the foundation of the world. Unite me with other believers who are sanctified and consecrated for your mighty work. Let my family and household members see Your hand upon my life. May they be moved to accept Jesus Christ as Savior and Lord of their lives. Now Lord, move me into my divine purpose and destiny.

I promise to give you all the glory and honor for everything that is accomplished from this day forward. I thank you, and I praise you in Jesus' name.

Amen!

Notes

Chapter One

1. Cole, Michael, and Cole, Sheila. *The Development of Children: Second Edition.* (New York: Scientific American Books, 1993), 648. For purposes of discussion in this text, the term "adolescent" refers to young people between the ages of 11-21. Psychologists in America further identify three sub-stages of adolescent development: early adolescence (11-14 years), middle adolescence (15-18 years), and late adolescence (18-21).

2. Ibid. Cole and Cole cite Larry Steinberg (1989), who notes that the sub-stages of adolescence correspond to the way modern societies group children in schools. Early adolescence corresponds roughly to middle or junior high school, middle adolescence to high school, and late adolescence to college.

3. Google: "adolescents + school + classroom disruptions + expulsions" or any variation for more information. Note that proactive school districts are now researching alternative methods which seek to identify areas of need in a student's life (academic, social-emotional-biological, environmental), provide support to the adolescent and their families; reduce time the adolescent spends away from instructional settings and ultimately further the academic progress of the individual.

4. Google: "dropout rate + underachievement + working class + middle class + upper class" or any variation for more information.

5. Google: "social (antisocial) behaviors of adolescents + community disruptions."

6. Google: "student achievement + effective intervention strategies."

Chapter Two

1. Begin your search for more information on these key issues with facts provided by:

    -   The United States Government at:
        www.usa.gov

    -   The *United States Department of Health and Human Services* at:
        www.surgeongeneral.gov/publichealthpriorities. html

    -   The National Institutes of Health at:
        www.nih.gov

Chapter Four

1. Google: "Civil War". "Reconstruction." Be aware of the fact that scholars have spent years researching this era and may report the historical facts from a variety of perspectives. The Southern historians, for example, would present a narrative that is distinctly different from that of a Northerner, an abolitionist, a slave, or a freed man.

2. Google: "timeline of black history/reconstruction."

3. The struggle for these rights continued for almost a century until the Civil Rights Movement matured in the 1960's. Many would argue that the struggle for meaningful and equitable political participation continues in new forms today.

4. Conduct your own research and develop your opinion on the following historical figures and relevant topics:

- The History of Public Schools in America

- John Dewy

- Carter G. Woodson

- Booker T. Washington

- W. E. B. DuBois

5. Google: "Separate But Equal" doctrine; "Plessy v. Ferguson."

6. Google: "Brown v. Board of Education."

7. Google: "Dr. Kenneth B. Clark and/or Dr. Mamie Phipps Clark" to learn more about "the doll experiment" and their life's work.

8. Refer to Note #6.

9. Examine the research and become acquainted with:

    - The lifelong advocacy of **Marian Wright Edelman**, Founder and President of *The Children's Defense Fund (CDF)*. Examine the history and mission of what is reportedly the nation's strongest voice for children and families. Read Mrs. Edelman's brief biography on the web site: **www.childrensdefensefund.org.**

    Celebrate and be inspired to learn what one caring person can accomplish for others in a lifetime.

    - **The National Urban League (NUL).** Established in 1910, and currently led by **Marc Morial, President, and CEO**, the Urban League is the nation's oldest and largest community-based movement devoted to empowering African Americans to enter the economic and social mainstream.

Study the rich history of this national organization as you browse the web site at: **www.nul.org**. Find out what the activities and initiatives are being spearheaded by the Urban League chapter in your local area.

- **Rainbow/Push Coalition, Inc.** The Reverend Jesse Louis Jackson, Sr., one of America's foremost civil rights, religious and political figures is Founder and President of the Rainbow/PUSH Coalition. Over the past forty years he has played a pivotal role in virtually every movement for empowerment, peace, civil rights, gender equality, economic and social justice.

Visit the web site at: **www.rainbowpush.org.**

Catch Jesse Jackson's weekly television program entitled: *"Up Front with Jesse Jackson"* currently airing on *The Word Network.*

- **Covenant with Black America (CWBA)** is a national plan of action to address the primary concerns of African Americans today. The passionate leadership of **Tavis Smiley** and a distinguished cadre of: educators, researchers, health and human services policymakers, legislators, journalists, and activists characterize our "21st Century Keepers of the Dream."

Visit the web site at: **www.cwba.org.**

*This is only a partial list of organizations and individuals who tirelessly labor for equity and equality in our United States of America. Continue to search for other organizations that represent your personal concerns and interests.

10. I invite you to go to the primary source, the **United States Department of Education** to study the origin and administration of the **No Child Left Behind Act (NCLB).**

Visit the web site: **www.ed.gov/nclb**

11. Updates and press releases on the **No Child Left Behind Act (NCLB)** and its pending reauthorization can be obtained at: **www.whitehouse.gov/infocus/education.**

12. **First Lady, Laura Bush** maintains a web site that encourages individual and community involvement for the betterment of young lives.

    Visit: **www.helpingamericasyouth.gov.**

Chapter Five

1. Read: *The Breaker Anointing* by **Barbara Yoder** (Regal Books/ Gospel Light, 2004).

2. If you have not personally studied the life of this often feared and misunderstood civil rights leader, you have chosen to be misinformed and uneducated on this important topic. I challenge your family, friends, and book club members to read and critically review the biography: *Malcolm X: By Any Means Necessary,* by **Walter Dean Myers** (Scholastic Inc., 1993). Myers has written many acclaimed novels for teenagers and middle-grade readers.

Chapter Seven

1. Google: "achievement gap."

2. Visit: **www.ed.gov/nclb** and your State Department of Education web site.

3. Google: "achievement gap + student achievement + race + poverty."

4. Refer to: **www.ed.gov/nclb** and visit your State Department of Education web site.

5. Visit **www.whitehouse.gov/infocus/education.**

Chapter Eight

1. Refer to Chapter Seven, Note 3 findings pertaining to: effective student intervention, effective instructional practices, (increase in) student achievement, effective community initiatives and family involvement.

Karen Kitt Ministries

Website address: www.kkministries.com
Email: kkitty2k@att.net

Photo Credit: Cedric Bates/Cleveland

www.ingramcontent.com/pod-product-compliance
Lightning Source LLC
Chambersburg PA
CBHW031251280526
45784CB00004B/1809